Manage your boss

How to build a great working relationship

A &

Revised edition first published in Great Britain 2010

A & C Black Publishers Ltd
36 Soho Square
London W1D 3QY
www.acblack.com

A CIP record for this book is available from the British Library.

ISBN: 978–1–4081–2804–6

This book is produced using paper that is made from wood grown
in managed, sustainable forests. It is natural, renewable and
recyclable. The logging and manufacturing processes conform to
the environmental regulations of the country of origin.

Design by Fiona Pike, Pike Design, Winchester
Typeset by RefineCatch Limited, Bungay, Suffolk
Printed in Spain by GraphyCems

Contents

How well do you manage your boss?

Answer the questions and work out your score, then read the guidance points.

How do you feel about asking your boss for help?

a) Confident that I'll get what I want
b) Confident that they'll listen
c) Worried that I'll seem like a failure

How do you feel about delegating upwards?

a) Not a problem!
b) Sometimes it's unavoidable
c) It's not really my place

How well do you and your boss communicate?

a) We clash fairly regularly!
b) Very well
c) We don't really 'get' each other

How do you react to criticism?

a) I hate being criticised
b) I welcome it—as long as it's constructive!
c) I find it disheartening

To what extent do you feel you can influence your boss's actions?
a) Totally b) Sometimes c) Not at all

How would you describe your network at work?
a) I make sure I know all the right people
b) I have a network of trusted colleagues
c) I don't tend to network; I don't have time for chatting

To what extent do you feel that your boss is working with you to further your career?
a) Not much—it's not in his or her interests to do so
b) We develop my skills and build my experience together
c) I didn't know bosses were supposed to do that!

How well do you think your boss stands up for you in appraisals and salary reviews?
a) I make sure they know what I want them to say
b) Well—it's important for the team that I am happy!
c) Not as well as they could do if I spoke to them more about my ambitions

How would you deal with a problem with a colleague?
a) Forcefully—they are being unprofessional
b) I may mention it to my boss if nothing comes of my attempts
c) I wouldn't

a = 1, b = 2, c = 3
Now add up your scores.

- **9–13:** You know what you want, but have quite an aggressive way of asking for it. See Chapter **1** for tips on communicating assertively, without being aggressive. If you have a problem with personality clashes, Chapter **5** should help you to reach a mutual understanding. You don't lack self-belief, but it can come across as arrogance and actually damage, rather than help, your public image. See Chapter **8** for a positive approach to improving your chances of promotion.

- **14–21:** You appear to have a balanced relationship with your boss, which is a great step towards a successful career. Of course, though, you will want to become a boss at some point: by following the advice in Chapters **1**, **2**, and **4** you will learn how to command more respect both at home and at work. Chapter **8** will then help you to hone your skills and progress in your career.

- **22–27:** *You* know that you have the skills to progress in your career—the trouble is, nobody else does, least of all your boss. You should learn to communicate more effectively—Chapters **1** and **2** show you how, while Chapter **4** explains how you *can* delegate upwards. It might be useful to find yourself a mentor; Chapter **7** explains the best way of going about this.

Communicating assertively in the workplace

Your relationship with your boss is one of the most important working relationships you will have. A positive relationship will mean that you're more likely to enjoy your work, stay motivated, and progress in your career. A bad relationship, on the other hand, can destroy your confidence and damage your career. This book shows you how to manage your boss, so you can each get the best from this crucial relationship.

Part of the challenge of any job is that you have to deal with a wide range of people, some of whom may be easier to work with than others. If you're naturally shy, or are unsettled by people who adopt a confrontational approach, you might find that you need some help when it comes to managing a difficult boss. Or maybe your approach is over-assertive, bordering on the aggressive, and you clash with your boss as a result. Learning how to communicate assertively—but not aggressively—could be just what you need.

Assertiveness is an approach to communication that honours your choices as well as those of the person you are communicating with. It's not about steamrollering your boss or colleague into submission—in fact, it's about seeking and exchanging opinions, developing a full understanding of the issues, and negotiating a win–win situation: one that everyone can benefit from.

By adopting an assertive stance towards your boss you are showing that you aren't a shrinking violet, there to be bullied—and, equally, that you're proactive without being aggressive or demanding. Later chapters will explain different ways of gaining your boss's respect and building a great relationship; but adopting an assertive approach is the first step towards ensuring that you and your boss set out on the right foot.

Step one: Choose the right approach

Becoming assertive is all about making choices that meet your needs and the needs of the situation. Sometimes it is appropriate to be passive: if you're facing a snarling dog, for example, you might not want to provoke an attack by looking for a win–win situation! There may be other occasions when a more bracing approach is the answer. It may feel as though you're being aggressive, but you're actually displaying assertive behaviour, as *you*, rather than other people or situations, are in control of how you react.

After a lifetime of being the way they are, some people are daunted by the prospect of change. But if you don't change what you do, you'll never change what you get. All it takes to change is a decision. Once you've made that decision, you'll naturally observe yourself in situations, notice what you do and don't do well, and then you can try out new behaviours to see what works for you.

TOP TIP
If you feel you need some formal training, look into some specially tailored courses so that you can try out some approaches before taking on your manager in a 'live' situation. This sort of thing takes practice, so don't pressurise yourself even more by thinking you'll 'just know' what to do—get some help if you feel you need it.

Step two: Project a positive image

✔ Use 'winning' language. Rather than saying 'I always come off worst!' say 'I've learned a great deal from doing lots of different things in my career. I'm now ready to move on and give my new job all I've got'. This is the beginning of taking control in your life.

✔ Visualise what you wish to become, make the image as real as possible, and feel the sensation of being in control. Perhaps there have been moments in your life when you naturally felt like this, a time when you have excelled. Recapture that moment and 'live' it again.

Imagine how it would be if you felt like that in other areas of your life. Determine to make this your goal and recall this powerful image or feeling when you are getting disheartened. It will re-energise you and keep you on track.

TOP TIP
If you're not very tall, it's easy to think you can't have presence because people will overlook you. Many successful people in all areas of life are physically quite small, though. Adopting an assertive communication style and body language has the effect of making you look more imposing. Assume you have impact; visualise it, feel it, breathe it.

Step three: Encourage others to take you seriously

As well as doing all you can to help yourself in terms of what you say and how you say it, you need to get other people to 'buy into' this assertive approach to communicating at work. Your boss will inevitably watch how you interact with colleagues. If your boss sees that you are treated with respect, he or she will treat you that way, too.

You can encourage respect through non-verbal as well as verbal communication:

✔ If someone is talking over you and you are finding it difficult to get a word in edgeways, you can hold up your hand to signal 'stop' as you begin to speak. 'I hear what you are saying but I would like to put forward an alternative viewpoint. . .'

✔ Always take responsibility for your communication. Use the 'I' word: 'I would like. . .', 'I don't agree. . .', 'I am uncomfortable with this. . .'

✔ Being aware of non-verbal communication signals can also help you build rapport. If you mirror what others are doing when they are communicating with you, it will help you to get a sense of where they are coming from and of how to respond in the most helpful way.

TOP TIP

Until you get used to being assertive, you may find it hard to say 'no' to people. (Remember: where appropriate, you *are* allowed to say 'no' to your boss!) One useful technique is to say, 'I'd like to think about this first. I'll get back to you shortly.' Giving yourself time and space to rehearse your response can be really helpful.

Step four: Use positive body language

✔ Stand tall, breathe deeply, and look people in the eye when you speak to them.

✔ Instead of anticipating a negative outcome, expect something positive.

✔ Listen actively to the other party and try putting yourself in their shoes so that you have a better chance of seeking the solution that works for you both.

✔ Ask about their thoughts and feelings by using 'open' questions that allow them to give you a full response rather than just 'yes' or 'no'. Examples include: 'Tell me more about why. . .', 'How do you see this working out?' and so on.

✔ Don't let people talk down to you when you're sitting down. If they're standing, stand up too!

Step five: Recognise different communication styles

There are four types of communication style:

- **aggressive**—where you win and everyone else loses
- **passive**—where you lose and everyone else wins
- **passive/aggressive**—where you lose and do everything you can (without being too obvious) to make others lose too
- **assertive**—where everyone wins

Remember that people communicate in a variety of ways. Your assertiveness, then, needs to be sensitive to a range of possible responses. Here are some tips on how to deal with the different communication styles outlined above:

✔ **Passive/aggressive people.** If you are dealing with someone behaving in a passive/aggressive manner, you can handle it by exposing what he or she is doing: 'I get the feeling you are not happy about this decision' or 'It appears you have something to say on this; would you like to share your views now?' In this way, they either have to deny their passive/aggressive stance or have to disclose their motivations. Either way, you are left in the driving seat.

✔ **Passive people.** If you are dealing with a passive person, rather than let them be silent, encourage them to contribute so that they can't put the blame for their disquiet on someone else.

✔ **Aggressive people.** The aggressive communicator may need confronting, but do it carefully; you don't want things to escalate out of control. Using the 'I'd like to think about it first' technique is often useful in this instance. The main thing to remember is that your rights, like everyone else's, need to be taken into account, including the right to say 'no'. Remember this when you are feeling badgered or defeated by someone.

Conflict is notorious for bringing out aggression in people. However, it is still possible to be assertive in this context. You may need to show that you are taking your colleague seriously by reflecting their energy. To do this, you could raise your voice to match the volume of theirs, then bring the volume down as you start to explore what would lead to a win–win solution. 'I CAN SEE THAT YOU ARE UPSET and I would feel exactly the same if I were you . . . however. . .' Then you can establish the desired outcome for both of you.

If you become more assertive, people won't necessarily think that you have become more aggressive. Be responsive to their communication styles, and their needs will be met too. All that will happen is that you begin to communicate more effectively.

TOP TIP

Once you become assertive, your confidence level will be boosted tremendously. The irony is, though, that you need to have sufficient levels of confidence to try it in the first place. If you feel you lack the confidence to assert yourself with your boss or colleagues, try the technique out in a 'safe' environment first so that you get used to how it feels, then you can start to use it more widely.

Common mistakes

✗ You go too far at first

Many people find that they go too far when they start to practise being assertive, and end up acting aggressively

---

by accident. Remember that you are looking for a win–win, not a you-win-they-lose situation. Take your time. Observe yourself in action, practise, and ask for feedback from trusted friends or colleagues as and when you need it.

✗ You're inconsistent

Be assertive across the board, not just with people you feel 'safe' with. If your boss sees that you give in when faced with an aggressive attitude, for example, they may adopt that approach when they want to get their way. Make assertiveness a habit, and you will command respect from everyone.

✗ Others react negatively to your assertiveness

Your friends and family will be used to you the way you were, not the way you want to become, and some of them may try to make things difficult for you. With your new assertive behaviour, though, this won't be possible unless you actively allow it to happen. If you find yourself in a situation like this, try explaining what you are trying to do and ask for their support. If they are not prepared to help you, think long and hard about whether they're really the right friends for you.

STEPS TO SUCCESS

✔ Try to avoid feeling resentful— if you are feeling 'put upon' by your boss or anyone else, act on the situation!

✔ Remember that sometimes passivity is the best approach. Judge each situation on its own merits.

✔ Speaking positively and using positive body language will encourage others to take you seriously.

✔ It is important to listen carefully to other people's opinions so you are clear about which points you differ on and which you agree on.

✔ Try your techniques out in a safe environment until you feel comfortable with them.

✔ Build up a toolkit of assertive techniques and responses that have worked for you in the past and reuse them.

Useful links

Assertiveness.com:
www.assertiveness.com
Businessballs.com:
www.businessballs.com/self-confidence-assertiveness.htm
Impact Factory (search for 'assertiveness skills'):
www.impactfactory.com

Developing your influencing skills

As workplaces become less hierarchical and more co-operative, working relationships are becoming based less on power and authority than on influence and persuasion. You have built your assertiveness; if you can boost your ability to influence, you will be well on your way to building a productive working relationship with your boss.

Influence and persuasion are very 'human' skills. Rather than telling someone what you think they should do, you now have to understand where their values, beliefs, and motivations lie so that you can influence or persuade them to meet your agenda. This is a sophisticated form of communication, and one which you may not feel is appropriate to your employee–boss relationship. However, most of us already do this far more than we realise; by simply increasing your awareness of what you already do instinctively, you will be able to develop your skills and put them to more effective use.

Step one: Aim for a win–win outcome

If you approach negotiations believing that if you don't win you've lost, you will undermine your efforts — either by being clumsy and heavy-handed or by giving up too soon and allowing the other party to walk all over you. You should see the chance to influence your boss (or any colleague, for that matter) as an opportunity to engage with someone who shares your desire for a mutually satisfactory outcome. If you have this attitude, you are likely to encounter co-operation and openness, and to reach a good resolution.

TOP TIP

Influencing does not require authority in order for it to be effective. In fact, influencing from a position of authority could be experienced as bullying. Influencing, done well, can result in both you and your boss getting what they need. If you enter the discussion with the intention of arriving at a win–win solution, you'll find that you have a lot more authority than you thought!

Step two: Prepare the ground

✔ Familiarise yourself with the situation and be clear about your desired outcome.

✔ Do your research properly: ensure you are properly briefed and haven't missed anything that might trip you up during your conversation.

✔ Before you embark on your influencing strategy, canvass the views of any interested parties. Forewarn them of your position and proposition and gauge whether they are willing to support you. If they have obvious concerns about your approach, you will at least have the option of modifying your position.

✔ Ensure that you conduct your communication in the right surroundings. It's best not to collar your boss in public. If he or she has the slightest concern about losing face, you will inhibit their ability to be open and flexible.

✔ Explain your reasons for conducting the conversation and outline what you believe to be the common ground. Check with your boss that you've understood the situation correctly. If you haven't, you risk undermining your whole influencing strategy.

✔ Describe what you would like the result of the conversation to be. When thinking about your preferred outcome, come up with a fallback option and be prepared to adjust your expectations if necessary.

✔ Emphasise your desire to reach a win–win outcome and check that you haven't missed anything.

TOP TIP

One size does not fit all when it comes to influencing. You need to put yourself in the other person's shoes so that you can meet their needs at the same time as arriving at a satisfactory outcome for yourself. When planning your campaign, you may have to put your own motivations on the back burner while you build an understanding of the other person's.

Step three: Communicate assertively

Assertive communication leads to win–win outcomes. It gives equal credibility to both you and your boss and encourages mutual respect and regard. Assertive language tends to be conducted in the first person (characterised by 'I' statements) and shows that you're willing to take responsibility for your own views and feelings.

Show empathy by demonstrating that you can see things from your boss's point of view. If you have difficulty doing this, imagine being in their shoes and experiencing the conversation from their perspective. What is it like to be addressed by you? How does it feel to be on the receiving end of the methods and techniques you use? Do you demonstrate thoughtfulness and respect? If you find it uncomfortable imagining yourself facing yourself, then it will probably be uncomfortable for them too!

Listen attentively to what your boss says and observe his or her body language to pick up any clues about what's happening for them and how they are feeling about the way the conversation is going. If you feel that you are getting resistance to your proposition, take a step back and create some space for reflection. It's tempting to seek instant gratification, but sometimes influencing takes time to mature.

Step four: Use a variety of influencing techniques

Below are some techniques you may come across. You may want to use some of them yourself—but others it's best to avoid!

■ **Logical argument.** This approach relies on presenting rational and reasoned argument to win favour. It works with people who are intellectually driven, but may not work in more emotive situations where values and beliefs are of prominent importance.
■ **Inspiration.** By creating a rich picture of a desirable outcome, you may be able to get your boss to buy in to your proposition. People who are strategically oriented and/or visually inclined often respond to this type of influencing style.
■ **Heartfelt appeal/friendly connection.** By reading and tapping into your boss's values you are much more likely to build rapport and gain co-operation. This

approach works well when there is empathy between the two of you. However, it can go badly wrong if you misread the other's motivations!

■ **Exchange of favours.** 'If you do this for me, I'll do that for you!' Bargaining can work wonders. Before you make the offer, though, make sure you can deliver—and then honour your commitments!

■ **Compromise.** A good strategy may be to meet someone halfway and gain sufficient ground to satisfy your needs. This can look weak if your compromise takes you into territory that you are unhappy with.

■ **Concession.** Making a concession gives the other party some ground, but also means that you can call in a favour in the future or ask them to make a concession in another negotiation.

■ **Blackmail/threat.** 'If you don't, there'll be dire consequences!' This is influencing through fear, and although it may be effective in the short term, it's not far removed from coercion or manipulation. Needless to say, whether it's you or your boss making the threats, this tactic won't do your relationship any good at all—and it will not build a relationship that will secure your future success!

■ **Power.** People who make use of power when influencing include those who dominate, those who are aggressive, and bullies. It also includes those who use referential power to get their way; that is, threatening the wrath of another who holds more power than either the influencer or the 'influencee'.

Step five: Close the communication

When you've reached a mutually satisfactory outcome, make sure that you follow up with written confirmation—and start acting on your agreement. You need to make sure that things can move ahead as planned, so make contact with anyone who needs to know what's going on. At this stage you should think carefully about what could go wrong and take steps to avoid any hitches.

It may be that you have to cut your losses and leave things alone for a while. Watch the other person's body language: you should be able to pick up when they have come to the end of their patience. It's hard to disguise these messages, so be aware of what's happening for the other person and take cues from their body language as well as from what they say. Don't push too hard or you will just experience an equal push back. If you start getting negative messages, leave things alone for now and agree to return to the discussion later.

TOP TIP
**Make sure that all that you expect to happen
is indeed happening, and that your boss is
doing what he or she said they would do.
Keep in touch with what's going on,
and step in again if you need to
help things along.**

Common mistakes

✗ You believe that if you have enough conviction, your boss will co-operate

It would be nice if this were the case! Generally, though, the more the influencer has invested in getting his or her way, the more they will have put off their audience. This self-defeating strategy has little mileage, so be prepared to spend a little time planning your 'campaign', and don't expect instant gratification. Think about what might be important to your boss, and remember that you might be working to different timescales.

✗ You think that being inflexible is 'strong'

This is a mistake. It is no good being stubborn and digging your heels in, as it forces the discussion towards a win–lose outcome. Be prepared to give a little as an indication of your goodwill and commitment to reaching a mutually satisfactory solution. If you don't, you risk undermining the respect you have built up from your boss.

✗ You try to influence someone on a matter that you don't believe in

If you don't believe in your proposal yourself, you won't come across convincingly. Make sure that you're fully behind the outcome you seek to achieve so that your communication comes across as authentic.

✗ You are too susceptible to others' influences

This can make you appear weak. Even if you think your influencer's views are correct and you would like to lend them your support, make sure you explore the situation from all angles so that they can see you thinking through their arguments and considering them seriously. You don't want to look like a pushover!

STEPS TO SUCCESS

✔ Influencing upwards is an important skill to learn.

✔ Remember that the aim of influencing is not about 'getting your own way'; it's about gaining a mutually satisfactory outcome.

✔ Be prepared. Find out as much as possible about the situation before you start your campaign.

✔ Strengthen your case by communicating assertively.

✔ Use the influencing technique that your boss will react most positively to.

✔ Listen to what the other side is saying and adjust your expectations/approach accordingly.

✔ Follow up on any decisions reached.

Useful links

1000 Ventures, 'Influencing people—The Art, Science and Practice':

www.1000ventures.com/business_guide/ crosscuttings/influencing_people.html

Impact Factory (search for 'influencing'):

www.impactfactory.com

Solutions 4 Training:

www.solutions4training.com/34

Acorn Coaching and Development:

www.acorncoaching.com/news.php?news_id=147

Organising your time

Part of managing your boss is about impressing him or her with your efficiency—which comes from great time management skills. You should make every moment effective by being truly focused and not dividing your energies by worrying about the past or future. However, it's still important to be able to keep the past, present, and future in mind so that you can plan and prioritise effectively. This gives a sense of order, structure, and security to your work, which means that you will gain respect for your efficiency, and convince your boss that you are indispensable!

Of course, there is also the all-important issue of work–life balance. If you organise your time well while at work, it is less likely that your work life will encroach on your home life.

In our working lives, time is the one thing that is in ever-increasing demand. Many tools are now available that offer instant access to information, the idea being that more time is released for increased efficiency and productivity. Yet although these tools are designed to save time, they can be so complex that they actually use up

a great deal of time and as a result put additional pressures on people.

Step one: Conduct a 'time audit'

As a first step towards organising your time well, do a 'time audit' on your life. What is the balance between the demands that are placed upon you at work and the obligations and pleasures that define your private life? Does this balance satisfy you, or do you find yourself sacrificing one activity or part of your life for another?

The key to good time management is being aware of the world in which you live and the interrelationships between the component parts, then choosing how you divide your time between each one.

How to do a time audit

1   Take a large sheet of paper and write your name at the centre.
2   Place words around your name that represent the demands upon your life. Include contracted work hours, travelling/commuting time, social hours at work—lunches, dinners, and post-work socialising— and family commitments, remembering that your time demands are likely to increase depending on the number of children or dependants that you have.

Also include your wider family and friends, sporting or fitness activities, socialising time, and time spent on hobbies or areas of personal interest.

3   Mark on the sheet the number of hours that are dedicated to each of these areas throughout the day. (You might want to use half-hour intervals if you think they'd be more meaningful.) For example, you might have: work (8), commuting (2), picking up children from school (0.5), and so on. This will graphically represent your life in terms of the choices and trade-offs you're making in those areas that are important to you.

4   Ask yourself, 'Is this how I want to live my life?' You may sacrifice some important areas of your life in the short term, but be aware of what happens when a particular phase of your life comes to an end. How will you manage this transition, particularly when it's unexpected or sudden, such as a change in work circumstances or retirement?

5   Take a highlighter pen and mark those areas on your chart that need attention. If, for instance, you feel you're spending too much time at work, you need to re-establish the objectives of your role and the demands placed on you by others. Perhaps it's time for you to think about requesting flexible working hours or job sharing, for example. Evaluate how you're going to get a better balance. Some of the time management toolkits outlined below will give you ideas on how to do this.

Step two: Be aware of your choices

The desire to improve your time management skills is half the battle, but you need to be aware of the choices you have to make. These relate to your overall life balance and the values you hold.

Look at what you're being asked to do at work and why. Is this because it's related to your role or because you have a particular skill or area of expertise? If you're being asked to do many things outside your area of responsibility, you may need to speak to your boss to clarify your job boundaries.

There are always choices to be made. You may find that you can win more time by working from home, thereby avoiding time spent commuting. However, make sure that your family doesn't automatically see this as additional time you'll be able to spend with them. You will need to create boundaries to ensure that your productivity remains high and that this new environment does not disrupt your efforts.

TOP TIP
Don't make commitments that you know you can't meet. If you're concerned about a potential time conflict, talk to the people involved rather than waste more time by worrying about it.

Step three: Plan for lost time

Look at your chart and see the effects of unpredictable delays and how they can affect the rest of your day or week.

Lost time accumulated over a period has a surprisingly large impact on the time available for other activities. You get a 'build-up' of negative time. If you can, plan pockets of space in your day to accommodate them. This releases pressure and allows you to get back on track.

TOP TIP

If you use any time management systems, start off simply for a better chance of success. You may find you have to manage expectations better. Build in some slack when you plan schedules so that you don't back yourself into a corner. Sometimes when people are aware of your timings, they build in slack as well.

Step four: Be prepared to change behavioural habits

Be aware of any patterns that characterise the way you manage your time. You may find that you're constantly overrunning in meetings or that you pick up a lot of spurious work because you aren't assertive enough in saying 'no'. All these consume time that you may not have available.

TOP TIP
Be honest about how long things take. Don't try to undertake the impossible or get hung up on process. Try to work with the philosophy of time management.

Dealing with disorganised bosses

In order for a team to run efficiently, every person in the team needs to know exactly what they're doing and how that fits into what everybody else is doing.

If your boss is disorganised, remember that it's not your responsibility to take up the slack. Instead, you must find a way to get him or her to stand back from what they're doing and look at their patterns of behaviour and the deadlines they and the department are working to. You could do this by asking for a progress meeting, ostensibly to check that you're doing everything you should. This will flag up anything that is being missed—whether by yourself, your colleagues, or your boss.

Often, time management requires a change in habitual behaviour. This can only be achieved by building awareness and charting a clear route.

Step five: Prioritise and plan ahead

Look at your workload and categorise your tasks into those that are important to your overall role, those which will add benefit to your role but may not be central, and those things that you do that you may be good at but which are outside your area of responsibility.

Set yourself definite and specific goals. What do you want to achieve in the time that you have? It's best to write these goals down. Make sure that they are achievable and set yourself a realistic time limit in which to achieve them. It may help to divide the task up so that you can take it step by step. This will make completing the task more rewarding, as you can measure your progress on the way.

We often get caught up in responding to others' expectations and sacrificing our own choices. As you undertake your time audit, make sure that you're not spending time on unnecessary activities that don't serve your purpose. Delegate downwards or upwards wherever appropriate (see the next chapter) but don't expect others to do what you can't do or pick up the mess you leave.

TOP TIP
Always plan ahead and try to anticipate the
pressure of commitments that you make.
Make sure that as you plan, you not only
build in time for reflecting and learning,
but build in time for yourself.

The central point is that planning is essential. It will help you prioritise, anticipate problems and potential conflicts, and see where you are going. Be aware of time pressures as you plan. Awareness must always precede action.

Time management toolkits

There are a number of time management toolkits that help people order their days, but their usefulness depends on the time invested in using them. Many time management courses teach you how to use processes to prioritise your tasks and activities. Remember that your view of what is a priority may be different from your boss's. In using these toolkits, remember to spend some time talking to all the relevant people to make sure that misunderstandings don't occur.

Some techniques and commercially available toolkits include:

- Smartphones, apps, and organisers
- 'to do' lists
- categorising work according to its level of importance and focusing only on the essential
- aligning tasks to business goals and objectives and cutting out the 'nice to do'
- shared diaries—team, secretarial, professional groups

It's not easy to make the transition from depending on a diary and Post-It™ notes to organising your life with a computerised device such as a BlackBerry® or iPhone.

✔ Plan the time it will take to learn the new technology and transfer your information. Allow a month during which you use a dual system, then throw the paper diary away.

New technology can be intimidating, but practice makes perfect. You will soon find your new system as convenient as any other you may have used in the past, if not more so.

Common mistakes

✗ You buy a new gadget that you don't need or want

In moments of desperation, people often rush out and buy the latest time management technology, which can be both expensive and complicated to use. It's always worth considering what is motivating you to make that purchase. You can't impose a new system when, deep down, you're not completely convinced it will help. It is much better to take time to get to the root of the problem and see what the cause is. Once this has been established, the best approach to time management may be identified.

✘ You expect too much of yourself and become disenchanted

When we try to change too many things at once, pressure is bound to cause us to step back into old habits. While the logic in time management appears straightforward, the complexity of our lives means that managing time is not straightforward. The answer is to take small steps, heading towards clear goals.

✘ You're not prepared to break bad habits and don't ask for help

How we manage our time can become habitual. We all know people who are always late or people who are always early. The way you plan your life and time rapidly takes on a pattern. Breaking that pattern can mean that we have to change the way we view both ourselves and the world in which we live—and ask for support from others in making that change. Speaking to your boss about your time management issues is not an admission of failure—it's about co-operating as a team to work more effectively.

STEPS TO SUCCESS

✔ Time management is about making the *most effective* use of your time, both at home and at work.

✔ Awareness is all. Being aware of how you spend your time, and how those around you spend theirs, is essential for good time management.

✔ A good place to start is to conduct a 'time audit', which will help to make you more aware of the balance between your work life and personal life, and between the different jobs you do in the workplace.

✔ Remember that there are always choices to be made—and be prepared to make them. Change the habits of a lifetime!

✔ Define your goals—this is an essential part of the prioritising and planning process. Make sure they are specific, realistic, and measurable.

✔ You can't plan your time down to the last minute. Be honest about the amount of time tasks are likely to take, and set aside time to allow for unexpected delays.

✔ Don't try to make all the changes at once—you will be far more likely to slip back into your old habits. Build them up over a period and you will soon see the difference.

Useful links

Mindtools.com:
www.mindtools.com/pages/main/newMN_HTE.htm
Total Success, Time Management training programmes:
www.tsuccess.dircon.co.uk/timemanagementtips.htm

Delegating upwards

Generally speaking, delegation moves down the business—but sometimes it's necessary to delegate upwards. It may be that you need to make use of your boss's knowledge, influence, or political 'clout'. For example, if a colleague is being obstructive, you may ask your boss to step in and ask the colleague to do whatever it is you need them to do. You may also find that on some occasions you need to 'borrow' power from your boss to resolve a tricky situation. Sometimes, though, it will be that you simply have too much to do and need some direct help.

As upwards delegation goes against the normal hierarchical grain, the methods you need to use are slightly different. In order to delegate successfully, you will need to find a way to motivate your boss to take responsibility on your behalf. Read on to find out how.

Step one: Tap into your boss's values and motivations

Delegating upwards is considered by most bosses to 'go against the grain', yet it is sometimes unavoidable. However, your boss is very likely to resist, as no doubt he or she will have a full workload too. So, think about how you can overcome this potential resistance by tapping into his or her values and motivations.

Motivational theorists generally agree that people build their self-esteem through achievement and recognition. This may be met through *power over people* or through *relationships with people*. Have a think about which of these two motivates your boss. If he or she is motivated by power, they will seek status, visibility, and credibility. They may put a great deal of effort into managing the politics and ensuring that they are in the right place at the right time, in order to raise their profile and further their personal cause. On the other hand, if your boss is motivated by relationships, they may spend a lot of time with their colleagues, building their teams, chatting around the coffee machine, and planning 'away days'.

Although the above examples are two extremes, it's useful if you can place your boss somewhere on this scale. Once you have determined which extreme they are nearer to, you can start to think about the best approach to delegating up to them.

TOP TIP

If you're simply being given too much work, one way of strengthening your case is to be clear about the effect on your productivity. For instance, you could say: 'When you ask me to add another task to my workload,

**I panic that I won't be able to finish
anything properly. How would you like
me to reprioritise my work?'**

If you feel that you need more 'clout', remind yourself that
most people like to feel that they are needed—especially
when it serves their purposes! Present the case rationally to
your boss, explaining your reasons for making your request
and emphasising the advantages of him or her helping you
out.

Step two: Consider your priorities—
and those of your boss

If you feel that you're being asked to spend time on a project
that doesn't make sense to you, try to see things from your
boss's perspective. This may help you to see the reasoning
behind his or her priorities. Take control of the situation by
asking for the rationale behind what you're being asked to
do, and explain your worries about the consequences of
putting your efforts in this area. You could say directly 'I don't
have the time I need to complete all my tasks and I'm
concerned that this will affect the way our department is
perceived. On this occasion, I think it would be a good idea
to pass some tasks back to you.'

TOP TIP

**Your boss may well say 'no' to you initially.
This may be an indication that you have**

---

misunderstood his or her motivations or have conducted the conversation clumsily. Try to remain assertive and repeat your request using different language and different reasoning.

Step three: Persuade your boss to take on the activity

If taking on your delegated responsibility helps your boss to move closer to achieving his or her aspirations, then they are more likely to take it on. There must be something in it for them if they are going to assist you.

1. **Reflect on your boss's motivations.** Do they enjoy wielding their power, or do they put relationships ahead of everything else? This will give you a clue about how to initiate your discussion.

2. **Set the context.** Try not to rush in just to rid yourself of a burdensome task, and not to be too emotional about the stresses you're working under. Ask for a meeting at a time when you can be sure that you'll get the time you need to explain the situation calmly and clearly.

3. **Be clear about what you would like your boss to do.** This means using assertive language. For example, you could say, 'In this situation, I will need your support and would like you to. . .' or 'If you want me to complete

my task by Friday, I will need you to. . .' Clear plans are far more useful than theories; and taking responsibility for your thoughts and feelings in this way will help you to communicate more effectively. It's harder to dismiss a human being than it is to dismiss an idea!

4. **Outline what's in it for them.** Spell out how it would benefit them if they took on the task. Use phrases like 'I can see that this will. . .' and 'I know that you place a great deal of value on. . .' As we saw in Chapter 2, you could even barter: 'If you do X for me, I will do Y for you.' Again, bear in mind what they value and where they invest their self-esteem. Be prepared to negotiate; think of a contingency delegation that would still take the pressure off and give you a sense of satisfaction and achievement.

5. **Listen carefully** to what your boss is saying rather than rehearsing your objections as she or he is speaking. This will ensure that you have all the relevant information you need in order to react coherently and credibly. And if you hear them say 'I will do. . .', you know that they have taken responsibility for the delegated task or activity.

6. **Ask for a follow-up conversation or meeting.** By doing this, you will make clear what you are expecting from your boss. It is also a cunning way of setting them a deadline! You might like to frame it as a developmental discussion for yourself: 'I'd be interested to hear about your experience so that I can learn from you.'

7. Appreciate their efforts by saying 'thank you'. As we have seen, everyone likes recognition, especially if they have put themselves out for you.

Step four: Stay confident and assertive

When you have this conversation with your boss, make sure you do so confidently. As long as it's in the best interests of your organisation, you have every right to ask for what you need. If you enter into the discussion with fear and trepidation, you will undermine your ability to communicate clearly—and clarity and confidence are what you are aiming for.

If you have worked through the steps in chapters 1 and 2, you should have no problem with putting your case assertively and persuasively.

Common mistakes

✗ **You lose your rag**

When you're stressed and up against tight deadlines with too much to do, it's tempting to offload your frustrations on your boss and even issue threats about what you will do if the pressure isn't reduced. This is no way to gain sympathy and support. All it does is create a view that you are a 'complainer', which will not endear you to any manager. Instead of venting your frustration, step back and focus on your priorities and the cost of not getting things done. If any of these are 'business-critical', take them to your boss with a proposed solution—which may include delegating some of your responsibilities upwards. If you can articulate your case reasonably and calmly, you are far more likely to be successful.

✗ You assume that your agenda is the same as your boss's

This happens a lot. Your boss's pressures will be different from yours, and you may be in danger of miscalculating where their concerns and priorities lie. Try to see things from their perspective before you attempt to delegate upwards. Remember your audience: it's essential that you make a meaningful connection with them so that you can make them want to help you.

✗ You expect to be knocked back

Not believing that your boss will help you can become a self-fulfilling prophecy. Delegate with certainty and assume that you will be successful. Present yourself calmly and thoughtfully and ensure that you have thoroughly prepared your delegation strategy. You may like to practise with a trusted colleague or friend. Brief your partner properly and ask him or her to come back to you with all the most difficult challenges. Once you have heard yourself go through the process, you will have a 'felt experience' to draw from.

STEPS TO SUCCESS

✓ Don't be afraid of delegating upwards: if it's for the good of your organisation, it's the right thing to do.

✓ Put yourself in your boss's shoes and work out whether they have different priorities.

✓ Prepare your case before speaking to your boss.

✓ Focus on the *outcome*, rather than the *process*. It is not the 'how' that is in question, just the end result.

✓ Present your case rationally, and don't get over-emotional.

✓ Play to your boss's values and motivations—and remember that flattery gets you (almost) everywhere!

✓ Remember to say 'thank you'.

Useful links

Businessballs.com:
www.businessballs.com
Time-Management-Guide.com:
www.time-management-guide.com/delegation-skill.html

Surviving personality clashes

What we call a 'personality clash' may, in fact, be something quite different. Each one of us has our own unique mix of attributes and beliefs that make up our personalities. If we clashed with everyone who was different from us, we'd be clashing all the time. Mostly, though, we're able to accommodate—and enjoy—differences because they don't threaten or undermine us. We can still maintain our own 'mix'. Indeed, our life can be richer and more exciting when we see the world through other people's eyes.

What is termed a personality clash, then, is often a jarring that occurs when someone challenges a deeply-held value or belief and thereby threatens 'who we are'; the person we present to the world. So, we fight to prove that we are 'right' and, because the beliefs we hold are such an intrinsic part of us, we fight hard. What we are really doing is seeking confirmation that 'we are right' and 'they are wrong', and trying to make sure that we don't have to change anything about ourselves.

Clashing with your boss can have a major effect on your working life—and your career. If you feel that your personalities are completely

incompatible, it's important that you tackle the situation before it escalates. This chapter will help you to put things in perspective and reach a mutual understanding.

Step one: Know what causes clashes

Personality clashes come in several different guises. They can be:

- **Personality oriented:** when people have different values and beliefs and different ways of expressing these. The classic personality types are introvert and extrovert, 'heart-led' and 'head-led'.
- **Role boundary confusion:** when the boundaries of each person's role are not clear. There may be an overlap or gap in responsibilities over which there is a dispute.
- **A professional difference of opinion or approach:** in a specific situation, people may disagree on the facts or on the best approach.
- **Irrational.** In these situations, people may express unreasonable **objections** to someone's race, religion, gender, sexual orientation, and so on.

There is nothing more frustrating than what is termed *l'esprit de l'escalier*: if you walk away from a confrontation and can't stop thinking about the things you wish you had said, stop and take a deep breath. If you feel that the cause of the problem is a personality clash, you are bound to take it personally because you feel that it's striking at everything you think you are.

TOP TIP

Take a step back and analyse exactly why you feel upset. Is your boss challenging one of your values or beliefs? Is he or she questioning the way you perceive yourself, or the value that you believe you bring to your work? See if you can examine the situation objectively to determine what is *really* going on.

Step two: Work out whether it's worth tackling at all

Bearing in mind that everyone is different, is it worth investing time and energy in trying to change someone so that you're more comfortable with them? They may have irritating habits, or even hold utterly opposing views to your own, but is this less of a 'personality clash', than something you should just get used to? It may not feel like it sometimes, but part of the value of going to work lies in meeting a wide variety of personalities. How strongly do you really feel about it? Is it really worth entering this territory and trying to resolve your differences? Are you trying to make them like you? Do you see your boss's different approach as an affront to 'who you are'? If so, ask yourself if it's reasonable to expect them to change just because they hold different values and beliefs.

And remind yourself that other people probably feel as exasperated about *you* sometimes too.

TOP TIP
If you feel that you've reached an impasse in your relationship, check that you understand each other's roles. Sometimes, we assume that what we think (or know) to be true is crystal clear to everyone else.

A common cause of conflict at work is when two people think that they should be doing the same thing or when neither person thinks that a particular responsibility falls on their shoulders. Both parties may believe that the other is being obstructive or negative when they are being nothing of the sort.

Rather than let these issues fester, break the cycle by talking things through and trying to reach a mutual understanding. Clarify who should be doing what, so that each party is absolutely clear about what is going on. It's helpful to follow up these sessions with a short summary e-mail thanking your boss for his or her time and summarising what you feel were the decisions reached.

Step three: Focus on what really matters

Rather than getting sidetracked by minor irritations, focus on what you can't live with any more. You will be investing time and energy in this process, and it will be wasted if it doesn't really make a difference. One way of working out whether or not your clash is worth tackling is to reflect on how much attention you give it. Do you keep returning to the same sticking point? Does it consume a lot of your time and drain your energy? Does it get in the way of your doing your job? If the answer to these questions is 'yes', continue with the next steps. If you can laugh off your boss's behaviours, then don't waste your time. It's rare that someone deliberately sets out to annoy you, so be prepared to accept that the situation may have emerged innocently.

Step four: Tackle the issue appropriately

If you do decide to talk to tackle the situation, do it appropriately. Find a quiet office or meeting room where you won't be disturbed and ask your boss if you can discuss the situation privately. Give constructive feedback by working through the following stages:

✔ Describe how you see the situation and ask if your boss shares your impressions.

✔ Describe what you see as your boss's point of view and ask if you have understood his or her perspective correctly.

✔ Show that you appreciate what's going on for the other person. Accept your part in the situation.

✔ Describe how you think things will change for the better if you manage to resolve things.

✔ Ask for your boss's reactions.

TOP TIP

Don't forget that you're likely to be part of the problem too! Try not to take the moral high ground; but be polite and listen to your boss's responses attentively and respectfully.

Step five: Don't get drawn into 'playground politics'

Apparent personality clashes, if not managed, can seriously undermine the creative and productive processes that go on at work. If people feel threatened by unfamiliar approaches and viewpoints, their need for validation grows and they may seek support from the wider community.

When you hear the words 'Whose side are you on?' you know that things have deteriorated and that playground politics are at work. People who pick sides often don't know what the core of the problem is and may end up lending support to people because of their power or influence rather than through allegiance to a cause. This development of factions will lead to a generally destructive and uncomfortable atmosphere.

Remember that everyone is unique. However, we often use our own behaviour as a benchmark and experience others' behaviour as positive or negative compared to this. It's worth remembering, perhaps, that any difficulties you experience with someone else are very likely to be matched by the difficulties they experience with you.

TOP TIP

If you feel that your boss is constantly needling you and that you're near the end of your tether, try to think about things from his or her perspective. Are you irritated because your boss holds a different set of values to your own? Does he or she view your role differently from you? Because values and beliefs aren't rational, they are non-negotiable—so any confrontation is only going to result in a heated and fruitless exchange of energy.

Step six: Agree the way forward

If you have followed the steps above, you may well have reached an agreement on how to progress from here, with some compromises and some concessions. However, keep the lines of communication open. If things become easier, thank your boss for taking the time to work things through with you.

Humour can be a wonderful way of dispelling tension. Once you have agreed the way forward, you may be able to use humour to prevent the clash from returning or to indicate when it is in danger of doing so.

TOP TIP

If you remain open to your boss's point of view, you will help to find common ground from which you can work out a solution. Once you get to the root of the problem, you can appreciate the shared territory and then focus on the sticking points. Keep a broad perspective and try not to get petty: there are some things that just don't matter!

Step seven: If all else fails, walk away

Sometimes people become entrenched in their own views and are just not prepared to change, whatever attempts you make to help them see the world differently. There's no point banging your head against a brick wall; in this case, just walk away. Drop any expectation that you may have had of your boss's behaviour changing and don't give it any more of your time. You will need to conserve your energy and time to focus on your own work.

Your efforts haven't been in vain, though. Dealing with personality clashes is a life skill that you will find helpful in many different situations. What you are doing is taking responsibility for your own relationships and communication and not expecting to be rescued. Although third-person mediation is a possibility, it takes a situation to an extreme which is more difficult to come back from. Try to resolve things yourself first and keep a sense of proportion.

Common mistakes

✗ You moan about your problems to the wrong people

When we feel low about a relationship at work, it's tempting to seek support from sympathetic colleagues—but beware of spreading bad feeling. This may make you feel better in the short term, but if people find out that they are being talked about negatively, things can escalate really fast. Try to find a trusted coach, mentor, or confidant(e) to talk you through your strategy for resolving the situation. Often, hearing yourself talk about an issue helps you look at it objectively and find a solution.

✗ You stick your head in the sand

Avoiding the issue and hoping that it will go away only leads to frustration and anger when it doesn't. It also means that people get angry when they should be trying to resolve things. Nip it in the bud by addressing issues before they become too threatening. You then have a touchstone to return to if things don't improve.

✗ You allow your personality clash to affect your judgement

This is a mistake. Make sure that no decision you make is tainted by your poor relationship. If you can't justify your decisions objectively, you are acting unprofessionally, and are in danger of getting into trouble with people further up the hierarchy. Ask a trusted colleague to scrutinise your decisions and challenge your motivations.

✗ You think it's all your problem

Remember that everyone—especially if they are in a line management role—must take responsibility for the condition of their own relationships. Encourage your boss to share his or her feelings about the situation, and give constructive feedback. If this fails, you may have to bring in someone from further up the hierarchy, or enlist the help of an independent mediator.

✗ You give up

It takes courage to deal with conflict, and many people are uncomfortable doing so. However, by taking responsibility for resolving the situation, you will take back control, gain respect, and build some life experience that will be useful in many other situations.

STEPS TO SUCCESS

✔ First, try to understand. This in itself may suggest a way forward.

✔ Beware of getting drawn into taking sides; this will get no one anywhere.

✔ Look at yourself through your boss's eyes, and recognise that you may well be part of the problem.

✔ Be objective—don't let a minor irritation develop into a major issue.

✔ Remain professional at all times.

✔ Don't let things get out of hand; nip any tensions in the bud as soon as you become aware of them.

✔ If you do talk things through with your boss, make sure you listen to his or her side too!

✔ Failing does not mean failure. Even if your relationship with your boss doesn't improve, you have nevertheless gained useful experience.

Working for someone younger than you

In recent years, the workplace has become far more dynamic. 'Womb to tomb' employment has become a thing of the past. Competence and added value win more respect than 'time served', and, in their hunger for self-sufficiency and success, younger people have started stealing the professional ground from their older counterparts.

As a result of these changes, it's not unthinkable that you will end up working for someone younger than you. It may take some adjusting to, but, by following the steps below, you can make it into a positive experience for both you and your boss.

Although there may be an increased possibility of conflict when people work for someone younger than them, it also offers many opportunities for a rich exchange of knowledge and experience. If managed well, the generation divide and the differences in attitudes can be overcome and colleagues can enjoy creative working partnerships. Read the steps below to find out how to keep conflict at bay.

Step one: Be open to new ideas and ways of doing things

Try to engage with your younger boss with an open mind and remember that their approach may well bring unexpected rewards and success. It is tempting to 'think against' the ideas and suggestions of a younger person, especially if you feel they are encroaching on territory where you have been successful in the past. However, try to stay open to different ways of doing things and explore the ramifications from a positive standpoint rather than a negative one.

Giving advice to someone younger than you can seem patronising if it is not done with care. If your boss is planning to do something that you have tried unsuccessfully in the past, try 'reverse coaching': ask a series of open questions that will help your boss think through his or her approach. Encourage him or her to speculate on what the likely outcome might be. By thinking the situation through in this way, your boss may well come to the same conclusion as you, without feeling that he or she is being patronised. You could then think of alternative ways forward together. Do remember, though, that just because something hasn't worked in the past, that doesn't mean it will never work. Something may have changed that will mean that the initiative will work this time round.

TOP TIP
If you're feeling uncomfortable about
your boss's approach, try to disregard
how your boss is doing things and
focus on *what* he or she achieves.
Don't get caught up in overanalysing
things; it just creates
unnecessary stress.

Step two: Be ready to learn

Although your cumulative skills and experience have
brought you to your current position, don't take the arrival
of your younger boss as a signal to entrench. It is never
too late to learn! Anyone who finds themselves in a new
situation will inevitably learn something from that situation.
Parents often learn from their children. Indeed, many parents
are heard to say that their children keep them young and
up to date. If it helps, see your boss in the same light and
be open to their perspective on work—but don't try to
parent them!

Young people have grown up with technology and have a
different view of the world from people who came to
computers later in life. There is much you can learn from this
technological literacy.

Step three: Don't make assumptions

It is very tempting to banish young people to the realms of the brash and the inexperienced. Try to see things from their point of view. Although they may look confident, they often have to work with people who have long-term experience and this can be really daunting. It is worth observing your young boss through the eyes of the recruiter and looking for the unique attributes that have put him or her in a senior position. Many young people are extremely talented and, because the age, class, and cultural barriers have largely come down, they often have an engagingly honest and open communication style which enables a free flow of ideas.

TOP TIP

If you feel that you are being sidelined by an overconfident younger boss, bear in mind that he or she may be overcompensating because they're threatened by your greater experience. You could offer feedback on your boss's behaviour, explaining why you're feeling put out. Ask what you can do to help, so that your boss knows that you are on his or her side and is reminded that you are a *team*.

Step four: Be proactive in your communication

Don't hold back when you need your boss's attention. Put an appointment in the diary and leave enough time to allow you to give proper attention to those things that are business- or relationship-critical. Try to make sure that any communications are two-way (no ranting or histrionics!) so that any exchanges are mutually helpful and productive.

TOP TIP

If you feel that your boss is making a mistake, consider the balance between letting someone build experience by learning from their mistakes and allowing them to crash and burn. Think about the consequences of your boss's actions, and if you think it will endanger his or her reputation and effectiveness, you may want to talk to them privately. Give positive feedback before airing your concerns and make sure that he or she knows that your intentions are good.

Step five: Be prepared to coach your boss

Coaching is not about directing, telling, or advising. Coaching is about asking open questions to reveal the dynamics of a situation and to enable someone to make sense of what's going on and come up with ideas. You can do this without wearing the 'coaching hat', but by using the questions to stimulate awareness and thoughtfulness. Hearing ourselves say something often enables us to re-examine our assumptions and decisions in a more objective way. By helping this to happen, you are making use of your experience, while supporting your boss in a constructive way.

Do be wary of investing too heavily in your boss's actions. There is a time to let go and let your boss find his or her own way. As long as you have tried to raise awareness of the situation and have acted in a supportive way, you have done your best.

Step six: Keep things 'light'

Try not to take things too personally. If your young boss misunderstands your sensitivities or appears to undervalue the experience you can bring, let it go or make a gentle joke about it. Let your boss know that you are on his or her side and that you are not going to be too 'high maintenance'. You are probably in a very good position to set the tone of your relationship, so make sure that your methods of communication reflect the style you would enjoy the best. It is amazing how much you can say in a humorous comment, as long as it's not too sarcastic or ironic—and as long as it is authentic!

TOP TIP
Reminiscing and telling 'war stories' is not always interesting or helpful! It is an indication that you are backward-looking and have a sentimental attachment to the way things used to be. Look to the future and demonstrate your forward-thinking attitude.

Step seven: Help your boss succeed

Your boss's success is your success. Try to be supportive and look for ways in which your boss can be seen to be successful. You may be part of a strong network at work, in which case spreading some good news about achievements will serve you and your boss well.

Change is always difficult because we have to let go of something familiar and replace it with something that is unfamiliar. It's important that you take time to rethink and readjust, as things can feel quite threatening during periods of change. However, try to look forward and see the advantages that the change can bring—and anticipate some unexpected advantages!

Common mistakes

✗ You feel certain that you know better than your younger boss because you are older and wiser

This can be a mistake. The value you bring is not your age, nor is it necessarily your wisdom; the value you bring is your ability to do your job competently. Try to see your new situation as a learning opportunity that may take you into exciting new territory.

✗ You feel that having a younger boss is a slight on you and your performance

If you feel this, you are likely to act and behave as if you have been slighted. You may think you are being subtle but your verbal communication and body language will give you away. This will inevitably set up a tension between the two of you, which will do neither of you (or your careers) any good at all.

✗ You reject new ideas from your boss

This can be seen as a passive aggressive act that is designed to make him or her fail. You may know of things that have been tried unsuccessfully in the past and you may resent going through the process again only to end up in the same place. Try to take a more positive view and help your boss to explore his or her new ideas openly and constructively.

✗ You assume that your boss doesn't have sufficient talent or experience to succeed

This is a mistake often made by more experienced people. Many young people have had the opportunity to gather experience in different contexts; the rise of gap years and sabbaticals means that they have often seen a lot of the world and had many challenging and developmental experiences, enabling them to bring a richness to their work that defies their years. Try not to judge your boss; instead, remain open to the possibility that they have an unexpectedly wide range of talents and abilities.

STEPS TO SUCCESS

✔ Appreciate the value of diversity.

✔ View the experience of working for someone younger than you as an exciting learning opportunity.

✔ Focus on the *end*, not the *means*.

✔ Be ready to learn and see things in a new way.

✔ Remember that you can coach without being patronising—as long as you go about it the right way.

✔ In some situations, people have to learn from their mistakes. Use your judgement.

✔ Always remember that you are a team, working towards the same organisational goals.

Useful links

Career Journal Europe, 'As population ages, older workers clash with younger bosses' by Sue Shellenbarger and Carol Hymowitz:

www.careerjournaleurope.com/columnists/edchoice/ 19940613-hymowitz.html

New York Post @ Work, 'What happens when baby boomer workers have to report to Generation "Y" bosses' by Hannah Seligson:

www.nypost.com/seven/08212006/atwork/the_rise_of_ the_junior_league_atwork_.htm

The Politics of the Workplace, 'The politics of being young on the job: managing the kid boss' by Ji Hyun Lee:

www.thepoliticsoftheworkplace.com/category/bosses

Working with mentors

Building helpful relationships with others can give you a huge boost during your career and can come in especially useful when you're hoping for a move up the ladder. As well as building your wider network of contacts, you may also want to consider working with a mentor, either from inside or from outside your current organisation. Mentors can be a great source of advice and encouragement, especially during fraught or tricky times at work.

Turning to your boss (or anyone else in your department, for that matter) for this kind of support is not always a safe or wise career move. Let's say you and another colleague have both applied for the same promotion. Clearly, your boss can't be seen to be helping one of you more than the other. You may not even have that great a relationship with your boss and you might be worried that this is blighting your promotion prospects. This is where mentors come into their own.

A mentor is someone who is committed to helping you find a path to success, helping you to gain the insight and contacts that you need in order to understand the steps to your future. He

or she should also be able to provide wise advice for your incidental crises and decision crossroads. Read on to find out if working with a mentor can help you get the career results you've been looking for.

Step one: Think through some common questions about mentoring

Can I trust my mentor to keep what we talk about confidential?

You should be able to. How else would you be able to learn, if you didn't have someone to ask all those questions you're too embarrassed to discuss with your boss? The ideal mentor–mentee relationship is based on trust and open communication. If you decide to work with a mentor, make it clear from the outset that you'd like anything you say to him or her to remain between the two of you.

What if there is no one at my company whose guidance I especially value?

Your mentor can come from anywhere: he or she could be a current or former colleague, or even someone you've met at a special interest group or conference. In fact, you can have more than one mentor. It doesn't matter at all where they come from, as long as they're not your direct supervisors or in your department, and as long as they have the insight and experience that you value.

Do I have to pay for these services?

No. Most people are incredibly flattered to be asked to take on a mentoring role and see it as an honour. Those who have been high achievers in their own careers consider it good professional 'citizenship' to help those just starting out. It's natural that there will be some people less willing to help, of course, but try not to get downhearted: see it as a reflection on them, not you.

Can I be a mentor, too?

Yes. Although you might not be high enough up the career ladder to be someone immediately marked out as a mentor, whenever you're willing to share advice and information to benefit someone else, you're fulfilling that role. Many organisations consider mentoring a valuable hallmark of leadership material. While you may be doing it out of kindness, others will take note and it will benefit your career in the long run.

Step two: Decide what you want out of a mentoring relationship

As with any scenario at work, you'll get much better results if you know exactly what you're hoping to gain. For example, are you:

- looking for guidance on building a career within one particular organisation?

- looking for help in developing your professional skills?
- looking for introductions into seemingly 'closed' circles of influential people?

The answers to these questions will help you decide whether you need a mentor within your company or elsewhere in your community or profession.

TOP TIP

Don't think that mentoring is a way of being spoon-fed useful information. The mentee has an important part to play in setting the agenda for the relationship and he or she also has to be in the right frame of mind to make it work.

Just as importantly, you have to think about whether you're the right type of person for this type of relationship. What could you bring to it? For example:

- Are you committed to contributing to the profession as well as developing your career?
- What will make the mentor glad to have invested time and energy in helping you along?
- Do you listen carefully to expert opinions and follow advice, or do you resist guidance?

TOP TIP

Some people are just no good at taking any feedback about their professional life, even

---

when it's meant constructively. **Be honest
with yourself; if you are one of these people,
having a mentor might not be for you. You
might feel under attack and the mentor
might become discouraged if their
advice were always batted back at them.**

Step three: Look for candidates

If you've decided that you would benefit from a mentoring relationship, you now need to find the right person. Let people know that you're on the lookout for a mentor in a specific area of your life and ask around for recommendations.

Also, check whether there's an official mentoring programme sponsored by your company. If one does exist, let the organiser know that you'd like to participate. Eligibility for mentorship varies from one organisation to another. If you're ineligible where you work, look for mentors elsewhere. Spread your net wide and think creatively. You could look for a mentor in your professional association, community centre, local chamber of commerce or service organisations. Your college or university may also be able to help.

Step four: Interview your candidates

It makes a lot of sense for you to whittle down your potential mentors into a shortlist and then find out the best candidate.

Don't take the first one that comes along, just because you're keen to get things moving. The relationship you have with your mentor will be a working one, so you need to know that you're personally compatible and on the same wavelength.

Let the candidate interview you, too, without your getting defensive or stressed. This is a low-pressure, getting-to-know-you step that, if done properly, will save a lot of time in the future.

TOP TIP
Remember that if things don't go to plan, you can end a mentoring relationship at any time. It may be that as your relationship progresses, you find that your views on life aren't as compatible as you'd thought. It's not the end of the world, so don't feel as if you've failed: just move on and appreciate the progress you've made anyway.

Step five: Establish ground rules

Once you've picked your mentor, it's a good idea to work out the basic practicalities of your relationship. Once you've got these sorted out, you're both free to concentrate on the task in hand. For example, ask yourself:

■ How often do you and the mentor want to meet?

- Does your mentor mind being called during the working day and/or at home?
- How often do the two of you want to review the relationship?
- How will you handle disagreements?
- If one of your goals is to meet people who could help you climb the career ladder, what will your mentor need in order to feel confident enough in you to start introducing you to his or her circles of influence?

Step six: Consider being a mentor yourself

Being a mentor is a rewarding way of building both your career and your profession in general. It can connect you with fresh ideas and ways of looking at the same old problems, and is an excellent way to network. As your mentees move on in their own careers, your network and sphere of influence expand as well.

Common mistakes

✗ You look to your boss to be your mentor

Avoiding this mistake is simple: just don't do it. If you've told your boss that you're hoping to work with a mentor, he or she may feel offended that you chose someone else, but you can explain diplomatically that it is common practice to look outside one's immediate circle at work to find a mentor. It makes a lot of sense and means that there are no conflicts of interest.

✗ You and your mentor become frustrated with the lack of progress made

In your initial conversations, make sure that you and your mentor share the same goals for your relationship. Also discuss your ideas on how quickly to expect projects to be done, and what kind of reporting system will work for you. The clearer you both are about *what* is supposed to happen and *when*, the less likely you are to have basic misunderstandings. Be prepared for things to go awry at times: not everything will work on the first attempt, but review your progress so far, and keep positive.

STEPS TO SUCCESS

✔ Understand what mentoring can offer you. It's an excellent way to benefit from someone else's experience.

✔ Mentoring is a relationship you have to work at. Don't expect it to lead to an automatic shoo-in to a top job.

✔ Your mentor doesn't have to come from within the company or organisation you're working for—in fact, it's probably better if he or she has some professional distance.

✓ It's best not to overcomplicate your relationship with your boss by asking them to become your mentor. Someone not involved with the nitty-gritty of your everyday working life is much more likely to see better ways of working or opportunities you may not have noticed.

✓ Mentoring relationships should be confidential. Your mentor should understand that, but it can't hurt to state this clearly before you start to meet.

✓ Mentoring is not something you pay for. If any of your potential mentors suggest that you should, politely decline and walk away.

✓ To get the best from this type of professional relationship, be very clear about what you're expecting to get from it. This will help 'frame' your meetings and help your mentor understand your personal goals.

✓ Do make sure—and be completely honest with yourself about this—that you're the right type of person to enter into this type of relationship. If you find it hard to concede that others may have a fair point or to take constructive feedback positively, it could be that working with a mentor just isn't for you.

Making yourself promotable

It's all very well having a great relationship with your boss—but part of managing your boss should be making sure that you are working together to further your career. A good boss will support you in building your experience, developing your skills, and making you promotable.

Being promotable combines your professional skills with your business sense and ability to build good relationships. This creates the impression of someone who will be valuable to your organisation at increasingly senior levels. Once you become recognised for your specialist expertise and have a track record of success, you're no doubt likely to be seen as a candidate for the succession line.

As well as your track record, however, the 'powers that be' will also take into account other personal attributes that go well beyond your current role. To get ahead, you'll need to demonstrate business acumen, political sensitivity, the ability to manage change, and loyalty to the organisation that employs you. These attributes go hand-in-hand with the need to communicate and network effectively and the ability to cement critical relationships with those who will sponsor and support you as you move along your career path—including your boss.

Step one: Ensure that you are considered

When competition is fierce, it's important to do everything you can to make sure that you are considered to be a suitable candidate for a new appointment. However, blowing your own trumpet too loudly isn't always the most effective way of influencing events. Being clear about what you want and why you deserve to be promoted is, of course, very important, but a subtle approach can also reap rewards. You could, for example:

✔ find a mentor or sponsor in the organisation with whom you can work (see Chapter 7 for more on this)

✔ discuss your development plan in the light of your conviction that you have more to offer the business

✔ observe those who have been promoted and ask yourself if you're displaying the same personal attributes.

TOP TIP
Try to become more visible by ensuring that
you take the opportunity to mix with decision-
makers and by sharing stories of your success
at appropriate times. Don't make too much
of your achievements or you may put off
the very people you need to court.

In some organisations, promotion is a thing of the past for all
but a very few people—usually in the senior management
tiers. These are:

■ **flat organisations** where there are fewer levels in the
hierarchy
■ **matrix organisations** where the business is
structured according to common activities rather than
discrete business units. Project teams are made up from
specialists across the business.

In such organisations, promotability takes on a new meaning
as there is often no clear succession route. There may be
prestigious and exciting areas to be associated with,
however, or some career-enhancing assignments that
you could target. Take a step back and examine the
patterns and trends of progressive career paths in your
organisation. Once you've identified the 'hotspots', you
can work out which suit you best and plan your approach
to reach them.

Step two: Build a winning personal 'brand'

Making yourself promotable is not an easy task because it implies a very wide development agenda. Aspects of this include:

✔ familiarising yourself with the broader business arena and general management issues

✔ developing social and political skills that enable you to build effective relationships

✔ finding a personal leadership style that you're comfortable with and that can develop into a distinctive personal 'brand' in the long run.

It's a sad fact that the personal skills and attributes that have carried you to the point in your career where you're looking at a more senior appointment are the very skills and attributes that can sabotage your success at this level. These include having too high a dependence on your specialist expertise, an individualistic approach that differentiates you from your peers, and an inclination to challenge the organisational status quo. Shedding some of these traits, therefore, may be the key to becoming promotable.

In addition to these features, research has highlighted several 'derailment factors' that can block an otherwise capable person from further advancement. These include:

'problems with interpersonal relationships, failure to meet business objectives, failure to build and lead a team and an inability to change or adapt during a transition'.

('Why Executives Derail: Perspectives Across Time and Cultures', *Academy of Management Executive*, 1995. Vol. 9, No. 4, pp. 62–72.)

Two further derailment factors that were considered to reflect the changing business environment were later identified. These were the failure to *learn* to deal with change or complexity, and overdependence upon a single boss or mentor.

If you work through the following steps, you can be sure that you'll be building the personal capabilities that will enhance your promotability and distinguish you as a future leader.

Step three: Develop good interpersonal skills

As you progress through your career, a shift occurs in the balance between the expert contribution you make and your ability to build relationships. More senior roles demand a higher level of political sensitivity because at this level, relationships go beyond the organisational setting and are more likely have an impact on the long-term viability of the business. Faced with this realisation, many potential leaders try to fake it with an overconfident communication style that conveys nothing but arrogance and authoritarianism.

Good interpersonal relationships are built by people who have no axe to grind and who aren't trying to create an illusion of confidence and capability. There's no substitute for genuine self-confidence; people can generally see through bluff and blag, so it's important to put the time in to really know yourself well, understand your values, and create a clear picture of what you want.

TOP TIP
Once you have self-knowledge, good communication and an easy manner will follow naturally because they will genuinely reflect who you are.

Step four: Meet business objectives

In order to make yourself promotable, not only do you have to meet the objectives of your role, but you also have to contribute to the wider business. This means showing initiative and taking an interest in areas outside your role boundaries. You could do this by volunteering for an important project, chairing a committee, or facilitating a special interest group. If you're seen to be supportive of, and passionate for, the business, you're much more likely to be noticed as someone who could add value at a more senior level.

Although it may be unpalatable to some, you could consider (subtle) ways in which you can broadcast your willingness to play a more committed part in the fortunes of your business, such as suggesting or volunteering for a special project. This doesn't mean that you have to be sycophantic, but if you act like someone who occupies the type of role you're aiming for, it'll be easy for others to see you in that role.

TOP TIP
While increasing your 'visibility' within the boundaries of your organisation is important, you don't need to confine yourself to just that. Why not publish articles in your trade or professional magazine, or accept invitations (or volunteer) to speak at conferences? If you want to raise your visibility more locally

---

to demonstrate your commitment to your community, you could get involved in local politics.

Step five: Build and lead teams

One of the essential skills of a senior executive is the ability to build and lead teams. Without this, the co-operative networks—which are vital to an organisation if it is to achieve its objectives—are damaged. Much of a person's success in this area depends on his or her ability to communicate clear objectives as well as understanding the skills, motivations, and personal values of those in their team. Relationships must be open, with a healthy ebb and flow of feedback to ensure that everyone is aligned with the purpose of the team. Milestones and markers need to be part of the plan so that progress can be monitored and successes celebrated.

Step six: Learn to manage transition and change

Business and organisational models change in response to developments in the market and economy. The ripple effects of these changes are felt throughout the organisation and have an impact on everyone. Being able to field such changes and use your knowledge and insight to direct people's creative energy towards making them a success are valuable attributes of a leader. As we have seen, entrenchment and other blocking behaviours are not perceived to be helpful, even if you feel that the change is unwise or counter-productive. If you find yourself in a situation like this, you may want to put alternative suggestions to your boss, explaining the thinking behind them. If your concerns are rejected, though, demonstrate your loyalty by remaining flexible and actively seeking ways of making the changes work. Show that you're prepared to remain motivated and learn from the new experience rather than demonstrate resentfulness or obstinacy.

TOP TIP
Remaining flexible, actively seeking ways of making (sometimes difficult) things happen, keeping people motivated, and learning from new experiences are all important characteristics of those in the top team. Loyalty and solidarity are values that are universally prized.

Step seven: Build an effective network of champions or sponsors

We've all seen people who have been promoted on the basis of who they know, not what they know, yet this is no guarantee of future success. Indeed, investing in a nepotistic relationship is all very well when your champion is in favour, but if their reputation is damaged for any reason, yours will also be tarnished because of your close association.

It's important, therefore, to build a robust network of relationships with people who will support you purely because of your potential and personal integrity. In this way, you can be sure that you aren't reliant on the perception people have of someone else (and over whom you have no control). For example, if your boss is particularly unpopular, by building a strong network outside his or her department, you will ensure that people know and value you for who you are, not who you work for.

Think about your network and identify role models, potential coaches, and mentors for different aspects of your development plan. When you approach them, be open with your request for assistance but beware of projecting self-interest above the interests of the organisation. Frame your request in development terms, stating that you feel you have more to offer the business and would appreciate their guidance.

In summary, being promotable does not rely on past success but on your ambassadorial qualities. Neither does it rely on overconfidence or bullishness. Being promotable demands that you demonstrate:

✔ an active interest in the business and an understanding of the strategic issues

✔ an ability to reach targets and build value

✔ a genuinely confident communication style

✔ an ability to build effective personal relationships, both among your colleagues and with your boss.

Common mistakes

✗ You irritate the people who could help you

Sometimes, people looking for a move up the career ladder damage their case by making so much noise around the people who they think can promote them that their efforts become irritating and counter-productive. There are unwritten 'rules' to being promotable and you need to work these out by observing and adopting some of the tactics of successful people who've gone before you. If your boss is one of these people, you are in a brilliant position to watch, learn, and develop.

✗ You're not willing to change

Although a track record of being a maverick may get you noticed, this is usually not a trait that will get you promoted. You need to play down your notoriety and redirect your energies into activities that are seen to support the organisation's best interests. If you're hoping to enter a different cultural zone in the organisation, you have to make sure you're familiar with the values that operate there and demonstrate that they're part of your value set too.

✗ You ignore your colleagues

It's tempting to focus on yourself as you look towards your career horizon and plan for your own success. You'll be judged on your ability to work well with your boss *and* with your colleagues, though, so it's foolish to ignore them. You won't succeed by backstabbing, so you must trust in your own abilities and help your team to flourish. Doing this will create a loyal group who will support you in your plans. Take care to maintain these relationships as you move through the organisation, as you never know who you'll be working with (or for!) one day.

STEPS TO SUCCESS

✔ Find ways to make yourself noticed without being boastful.

✔ Familiarise yourself with the skills necessary to succeed in your workplace and work hard at developing these.

✔ Build good personal relationships and be aware of others' needs.

✔ Expand your capabilities outside your specific role—take an interested and active part in the wider business of your company.

✔ Refine your leadership skills and learn to be flexible and accommodating of change.

✔ Work with those around you to support your cause. This means not only building up a contact network but being cautious not to offend existing and potential colleagues.

Useful links

Promotion Quiz:
http://money.cnn.com/popups/2006/fortune/quizzes/ promotion/1q.html
iVillage.co.uk:
www.ivillage.co.uk/workcareer/survive/archive/ 0,,156470,00.html
Career-Success-For-Newbies.com:
www.career-success-for-newbies.com/how-to-get- promoted.html
FabJob.com:
www.fabjob.com/tips125.html

Where to find more help

The Art of Persuasion: How to Influence People and Get What You Want
Juliet Erickson
Hodder Mobius, 2005
256pp ISBN 034083031X
We all know what we want—it's getting it that's the problem! Full of constructive, easy-to-apply advice, this book helps the reader to build understanding and plan the best, most effective approach. The advice in the book can be applied in both business and personal situations.

Leading Self-Directed Work Teams: A Guide to Developing New Team Leadership Skills: 2nd ed.
Kimball Fisher
McGraw-Hill, 2000
339pp ISBN 0071349243
In this book the author describes the change in roles between management and employees that must occur for self-directed work teams (SDWTs) to succeed. He discusses how management may see SDWTs as a threat and how supervisors need to rethink their role. He looks at situations where SDWTs are being used and also explains how technology is causing the number of SDWTs to increase.

The Nice Factor: The Art of Saying No
Jo Ellen Gryzb and Robin Chandler
Fusion Press, 2008
256pp ISBN 1905745362
Many of us equate being nice with being a good person, but 'nice' people find often themselves frustrated and inhibited, unable to say 'no' to others or to truly speak their minds. This groundbreaking guide will put you back in control by teaching you how to act with confidence, express your needs and wants and assert yourself in every aspect of your life.

Getting It Done: How to Lead When You're *Not* in Charge
Roger Fisher and Alan Sharp
HarperBusiness, 1999
240pp ISBN 0887309585

Packed with useful advice, techniques, and action plans, *Getting It Done* is about getting people in your organisation to adjust their habits, perspective, and behaviour and 'buy in' to progress. The authors look at how 'lateral leadership' (that is, influencing your peers) provides lessons for when you are yourself the boss. They help you to see yourself as both part of the problem and part of the solution, and suggest what skills you could improve, and how you can influence people in such a way that will lead to genuine, effective progress.

Coaching for Leadership: The Practice of Leadership Coaching from the World's Greatest Coaches: 2nd ed.
Marshall Goldsmith and Laurence S. Lyons
Pfeiffer, 2005
288pp ISBN 0787977632

This second edition updates and expands on the original, which has become a classic in the field of executive coaching. It brings together the thinking of a number of experienced coaches with the aim of giving both an insight into the importance of coaching as a route to leadership and an understanding of what can be achieved through coaching. Intended for anyone who provides or receives coaching, it explains the foundations of coaching, the roles adopted by those who participate in it, and coaching situations that arise from moments of transition, besides examining the practice and techniques involved. A number of case studies are included.

Influencing Within Organizations: 2nd ed.

Andrzej Huczynski
Routledge, 2004
408pp, ISBN 0415311632

There are many 'how-to' books on influencing, but few are based on rigorous research. There are also many academic studies, but they tend to offer little in the way of practical advice. Made up of a combination of up-to-date theory and practical step-by-step advice, *Influencing Within Organizations* helps readers to develop this crucial skill. The author looks at verbal and non-verbal influencing, impression management, networking, influencing in a group, and public speaking.

How People Tick: A Guide to Over 50 Types of Difficult People and How to Handle Them: 2nd revised ed.

Mike Leibling
Kogan Page, 2009
208pp ISBN 0749454598

How People Tick is a practical guide which explains how best to handle over 50 types of difficult people. Among others, it will help you deal with people who are angry, anxious, boring, bullies, competitive, hostile, indecisive, insecure, moody, negative, patronising, selfish, stressed, unassertive, unmotivated, or workaholics. It describes each type of difficult behaviour, looks at why it happens, and offers constructive advice for dealing with the problem.

Powerful Women: Dancing on the Glass Ceiling

Sam Parkhouse
Wiley, 2001
256pp ISBN 0471499056

This very readable book, written in a popular magazine style, focuses on the individual stories behind the successes of several unusual women. It is aimed at a very general audience and takes neither an academic nor an equal opportunities perspective but attempts to get to grips with the real experiences of case study women, such as Barbara Cassani, Belinda Earl, Nicola Horlick, Anita Roddick, and Margaret Jay.

Persuasion: The Art of Influencing People: 2nd ed.
James Borg
Prentice Hall, 2007
267pp, ISBN 0273712993
The second edition of this best-selling book shows you how to get
other people to do what you want through a set of golden
behavioural rules. Learn the power of words, how to be an effective
listener, how to enhance your memory, how to control the attention
of others and how to read body language and other non-verbal
signs so that you can achieve more in every area of your personal
and professional life.

Effective Leadership: How to be a Successful Leader: New revised ed.
John Adair
Pan, 2009
240pp, ISBN 0330504193
In this new revised edition, John Adair, Britain's foremost expert on
leadership training, shows how every manager can learn to lead.
Drawing on numerous examples of leadership in action –
commercial, historical, military – he identifies the characteristics and
skills you need to be an effective leader and explains how you can
enhance your personality, knowledge and position to become the
best leader you can be.

What Got You Here Won't Get You There: How Successful People Become Even More Successful
Marshall Goldsmith
Profile Books, 2008
256pp, ISBN 1846681375
This self-help is aimed at executives and managers who wish to
improve their 'soft skills' and other interpersonal traits. The attitudes
and behaviours that got you where you are in the workplace might
not be appropriate in a world that is changing around you, so it's
important to take a good objective look at yourself every now and
again. The author not only describes what you must do better, but
also explains the importance of consciously *not* doing certain things
which get in the way of your success.